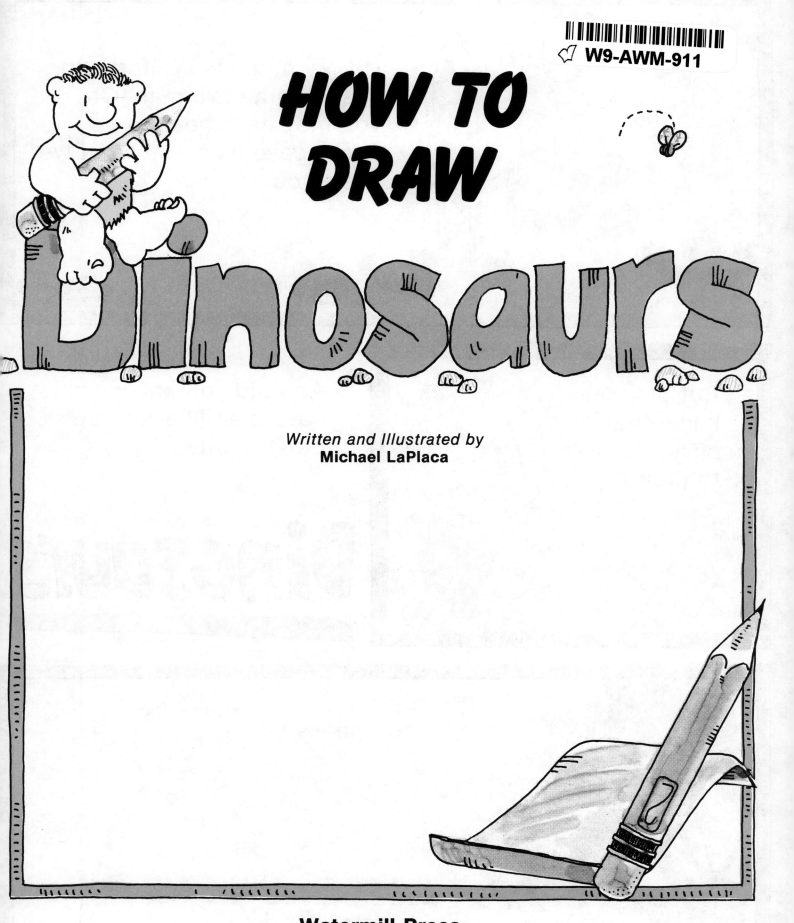

HOW TO DRAW
Dinosaurs

Written and Illustrated by
Michael LaPlaca

Watermill Press

Although dino-saurs lived a long time ago, they have not been forgotten, and they are still very interesting.

anyway...

What I'm here to talk to you about is drawing dinosaurs.

Dinosaurs are a lot of fun to draw, and they also have some funny names...

(and some scary names, too).

We'll begin to draw very soon, but first we'll have to get some supplies together.

3

Materials...

The first things you'll need are some pencils. I like to use Number 2 pencils. Make sure they are sharp (but be careful with them).

You'll also need some paper (a pad is good),

an eraser,

crayons,

a scissors,

some construction paper,

and tape or glue.

Basic Shapes

Here are a few basic shapes you should practice drawing before you start. You'll find that these shapes are used again and again to start your drawings.

First, there is the circle:

Next, to make up most of the shapes in this book, you will need to draw lots of ovals and other fun shapes like these:

The next shape is the triangle: But you are going to use rounded triangles like these:

Next, there are two three-dimensional shapes. They are

the cone: and the cylinder:

You will need these shapes to draw dinosaur tails and legs. Practice drawing all these shapes on a separate piece of paper before you begin.

After you have finished drawing the dinosaurs, you might like to carefully cut them out with scissors and glue or tape them to brightly colored construction paper. You can create a whole scene by drawing trees and plants. Placing several dinosaurs together on the same page also looks nice. Have fun!

Triceratops

(try-SER-uh-tops)

This is what your finished drawing will look like. Just follow the steps on the next page and you will see how easily it can be drawn. For all the drawings in this book, use your crayons to add the final shading and details to your dinosaurs.

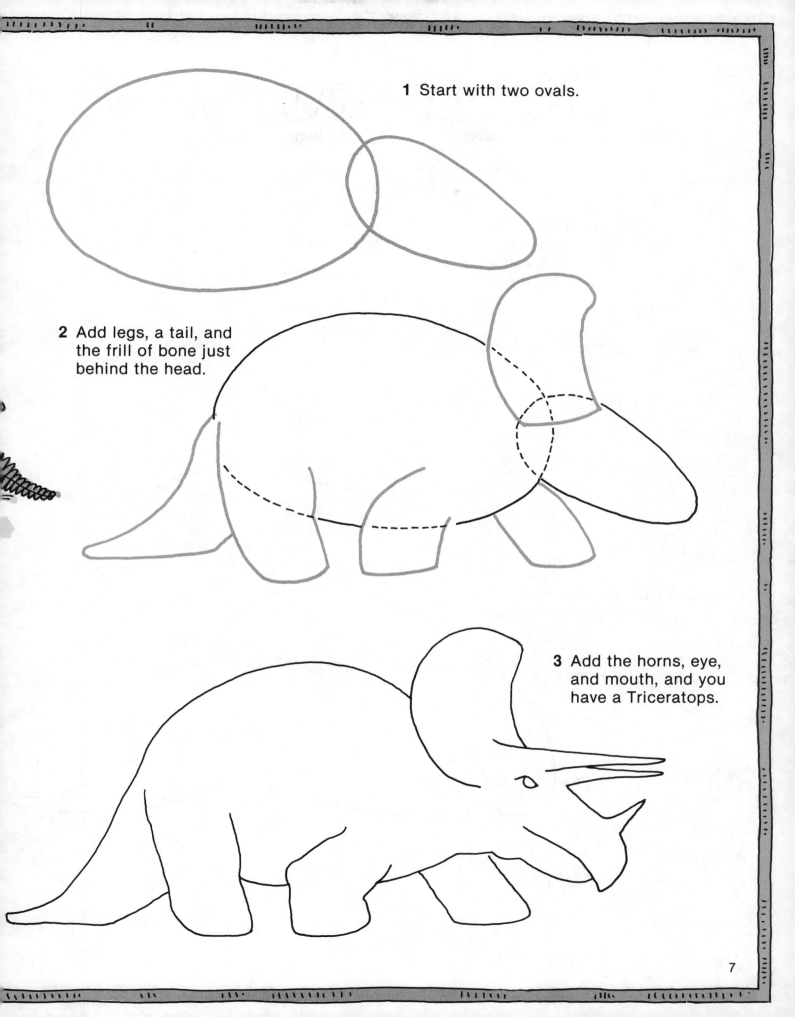

1 Start with two ovals.

2 Add legs, a tail, and the frill of bone just behind the head.

3 Add the horns, eye, and mouth, and you have a Triceratops.

Stegosaurus

(steg-uh-SAWR-us)

1 Start with ovals for
the head and body.
Add the neck and a
long cone for the tail.

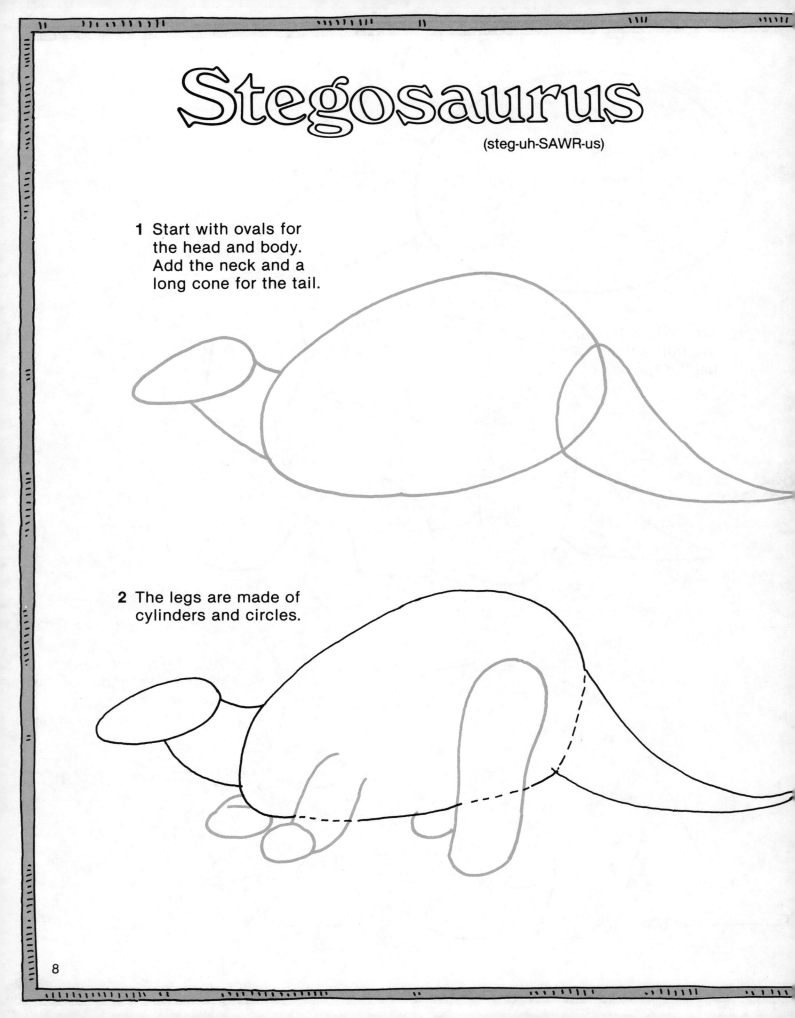

2 The legs are made of
cylinders and circles.

3 Try drawing one of the bone plates. Then add them to your drawing.

Stegosaurus had large plates of bone that came out of its back. They were probably used as protection from enemies.

4 Add the eye, mouth, and nose. Don't forget to add the sharp spikes at the end of the Stegosaurus's tail.

Stegosaurus was about 20 feet (6 meters) long.

Brontosaurus

(bron-tuh-SAWR-us)

1 Draw ovals for the head and body and connect them with the neck.

2 Add the tail and legs. Then add the eye and mouth.

Brontosaurus was a giant dinosaur. Its name means "thunder lizard." When Brontosaurus walked, the ground must have shaken like thunder. It was about 70 feet (21 meters) long and weighed 30 tons (27 metric tons).

Diplodocus

(dih-PLAH-duh-kuss)

Diplodocus was the longest animal ever to walk the Earth. It was almost 90 feet (27 meters) from head to tail and was a plant-eater.

1 Diplodocus looks very much like the Brontosaurus, so start with a head, neck, and body.

2 Add the legs and tail.

3 Then add the eye, nose, and mouth.

Brachiosaurus

(brack-ee-oh-SAWR-us)

1 Like Brontosaurus and Diplodocus, start with the head, neck, and body.

2 Add the legs and tail. Don't forget the eye, nose, mouth, and the air hole on the top of the head.

Air hole

Brachiosaurus was the heaviest of all dinosaurs. It weighed as much as 75 tons (68 metric tons). That's more than twenty average-sized cars. It used the air hole on its head to breathe when it went into deep water.

Trachodon

(TRACK-uh-don)

Trachodon was a gentle plant-eater about 30 feet (9 meters) long. It had a ducklike bill and over a thousand teeth in its mouth.

1 Start with three shapes that look like this.

2 Connect them and add a tail.

3 Add the arms, legs, eye, and mouth.

Ankylosaurus

(an-kill-uh-SAWR-us)

1 Draw two shapes that look like this.

2 Add legs and a tail with a bony club at the end.

Practice drawing a spike in two steps.

3 Draw an eye, a mouth, and two cone-shaped horns on its head.

Ankylosaurus had an armored "shell" something like a turtle's. It had many spikes and was about 15 feet (5 meters) long.

Allosaurus

(al-uh-SAWR-us)

1 Start with three ovals.

2 Connect the ovals and add arms, legs, and the tail.

3 Add the mouth.

4 Add the eye and the nostril.

5 Add the terrible teeth.

Add the claws.

Allosaurus could run very fast as it chased its prey. It was about 35 feet (11 meters) long.

Did you know that the word *dinosaur* means "terrible lizard"? Allosaurus was a very terrible dinosaur.

Tyrannosaurus
(tie-ran-uh-SAWR-us)

1 Start with these two shapes for the head and body.

2 Add the powerful tail, the legs, and small arms.

3 Now draw the claws. They are very sharp.

The feet look very much like the Allosaurus's.

4 Add the mouth, teeth, and eye.

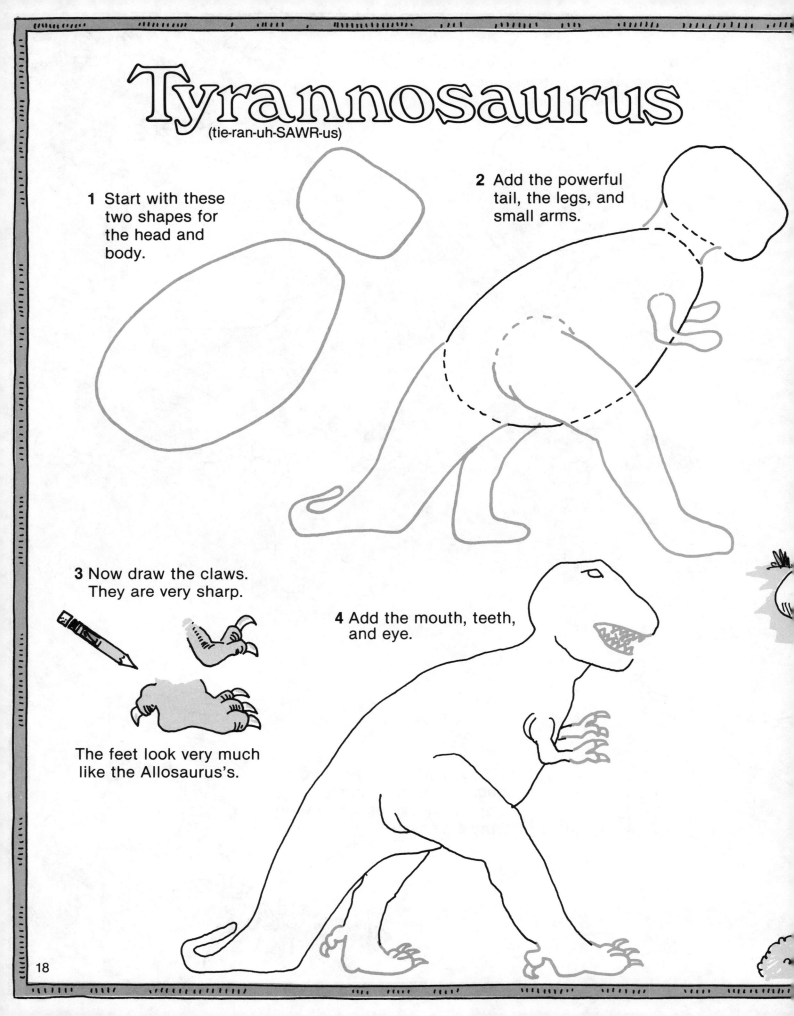

Tyrannosaurus was over 50 feet (15 meters) long and was taller than a two-story house. It had a fierce leathery hide.

Tyrannosaurus means "tyrant lizard." It was the largest meat-eater that ever lived.

Deinonychus

(DIE-no-ni-kuss)

1 Start with these oval shapes.

2 Add arms, legs, and a tail.

Deinonychus was a small meat-eater, but very fierce. Deinonychus is sometimes called "terrible claw."

3 Deinonychus had claws that were similar to Allosaurus's.

4 Add the mouth, teeth, nostril, and eye.

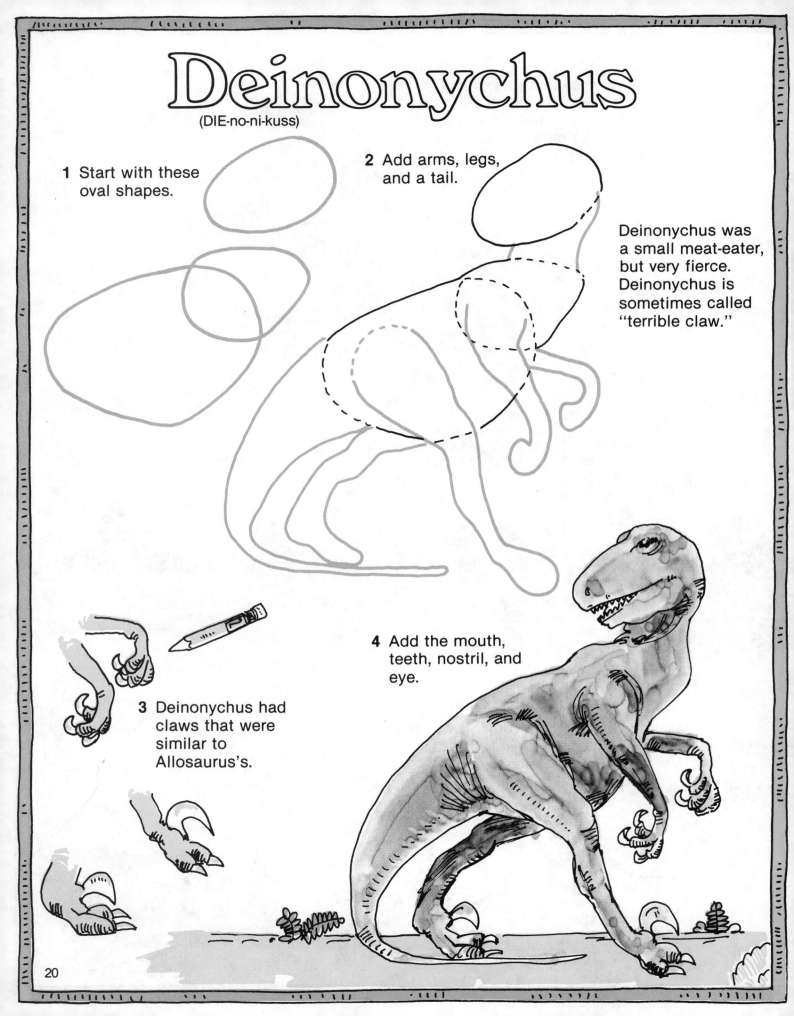

Ornithosuchus

(or-ni-THOH-sue-kuss)

1 Start with three ovals.

Ornithosuchus had a bony ridge down the center of its back. It was one of the first meat-eating dinosaurs.

Triassic

2 Add arms, legs, neck, and tail.

3 Add the eye, nose, and mouth.

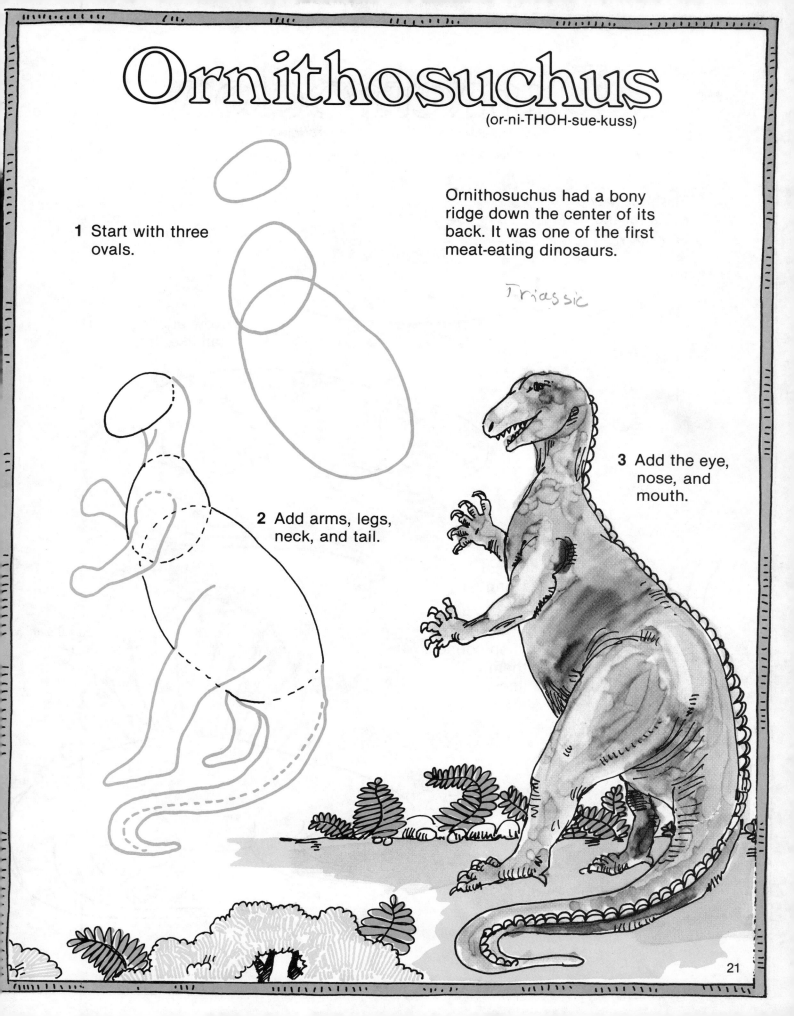

21

Dimetrodon
(die-MET-ruh-don)

1 First, draw two ovals for the head and body.

2 Now add legs and a tail like this.

3 Draw the "dorsal sail" by drawing vertical spokes.

Then connect them with curved lines.

Dorsal sail

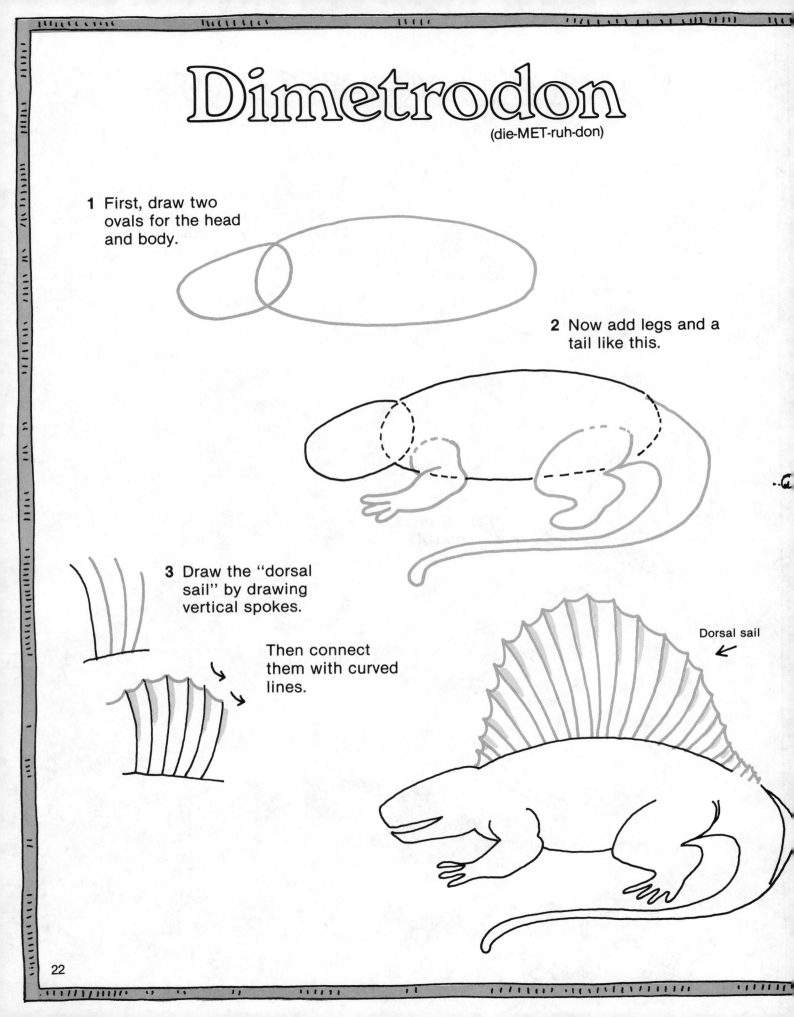

The large dorsal sail on Dimetrodon's back may have helped this dinosaur to stay cool when it was hot and warm when it was cold.

4 Don't forget the eye, nostril, and teeth.

Hidden eggs

Most dinosaur babies were hatched from eggs. The dinosaurs had to hide their eggs so that other dinosaurs would not eat them.

Elasmosaurus
(ee-laz-muh-SAWR-us)

1 Start with two ovals and connect them with a long neck.

2 Add a long tail and "paddles" instead of legs.

3 Then add the mouth, teeth, eye, and nose.

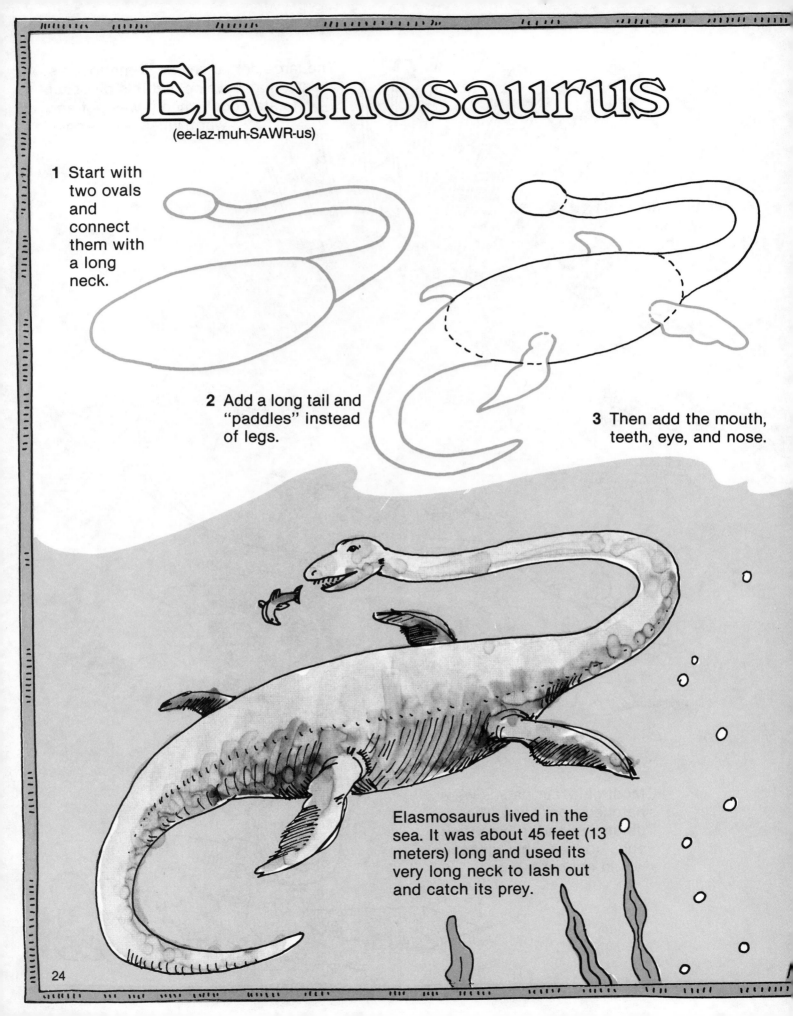

Elasmosaurus lived in the sea. It was about 45 feet (13 meters) long and used its very long neck to lash out and catch its prey.

Kronosaurus

(kron-uh-SAWR-us)

1 Start with two overlapping ovals.

2 Add the powerful tail and "paddle" legs.

3 Don't forget the eye, the mouth, and the sharp teeth.

Kronosaurus was about 55 feet (16 meters) long. Although it lived in the sea, it might have been able to scramble about on land by using its strong paddle legs.

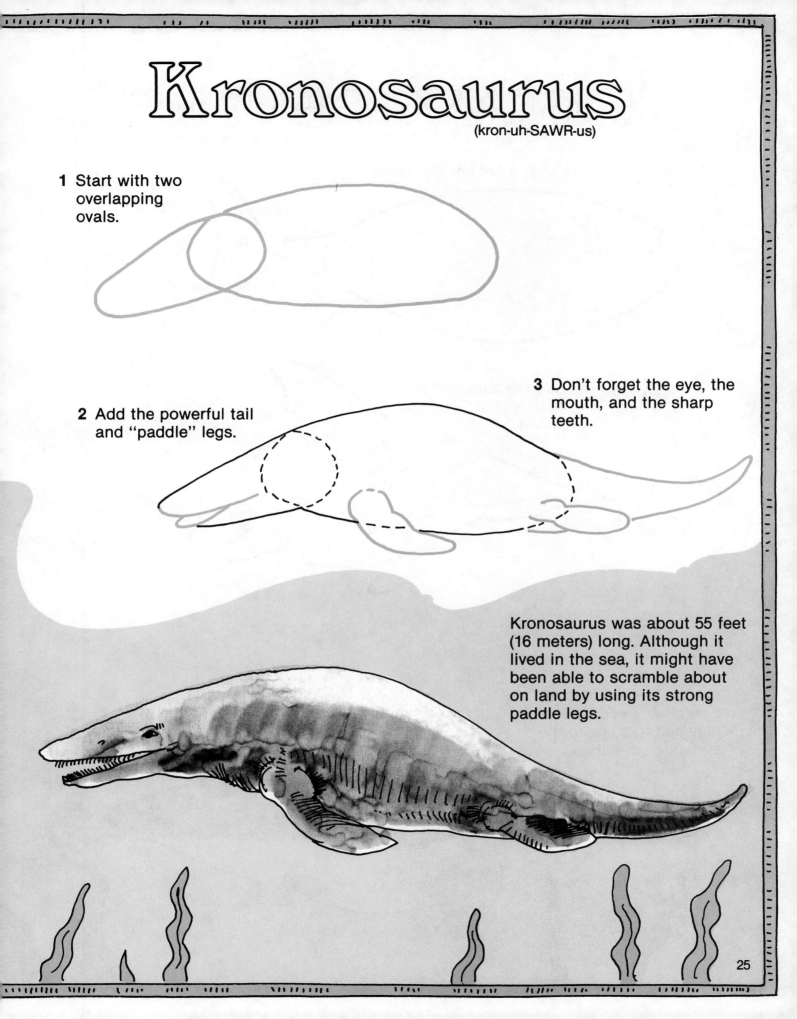

Ichthyosaurus

(ik-thee-uh-SAWR-us)

1 Start with an oval and a tail like this.

2 Add the nose and fins. Then add the eye and mouth.

Ichthyosaurus looked something like the dolphins of today. They grew to be about 10 feet (3 meters) long. Like other sea dinosaurs, they had to come to the surface to breathe.

Tylosaurus

(tie-luh-SAWR-us)

1 Start with an oval and a rounded triangle.

2 Add the long nose, lower jaw, tail, and paddles. Then add the teeth, eye, and the fins on the tail and back.

Tylosaurus was a fierce sea monster. Its lower jaw had a special hinge that allowed it to open wide and swallow huge fish.

Rhamphorhynchus

(ram-fuh-RINK-us)

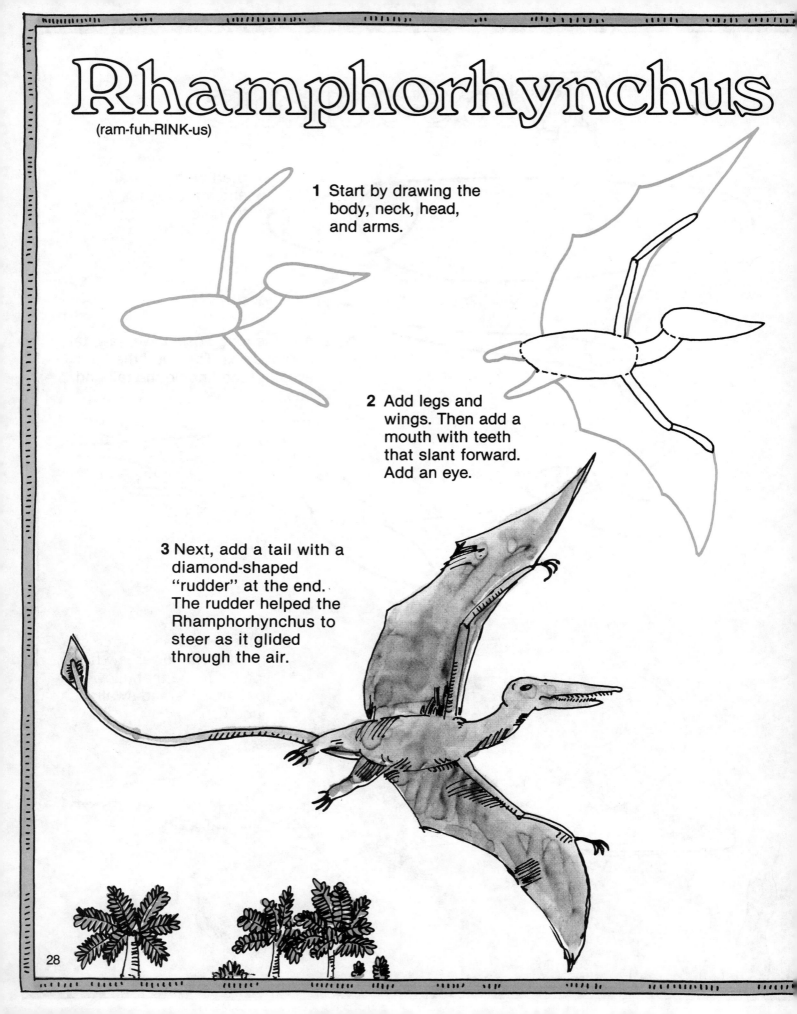

1 Start by drawing the body, neck, head, and arms.

2 Add legs and wings. Then add a mouth with teeth that slant forward. Add an eye.

3 Next, add a tail with a diamond-shaped "rudder" at the end. The rudder helped the Rhamphorhynchus to steer as it glided through the air.

Pteranodon

(tuh-RAN-uh-don)

1 Start by drawing the body, neck, head, and arms.

2 Add the legs and wings. Add the open mouth and eye.

The Pteranodon was huge. Its wingspan sometimes reached 50 feet (15 meters) from tip to tip. It had no teeth and its diet consisted mainly of fish, which it caught with its long beak.

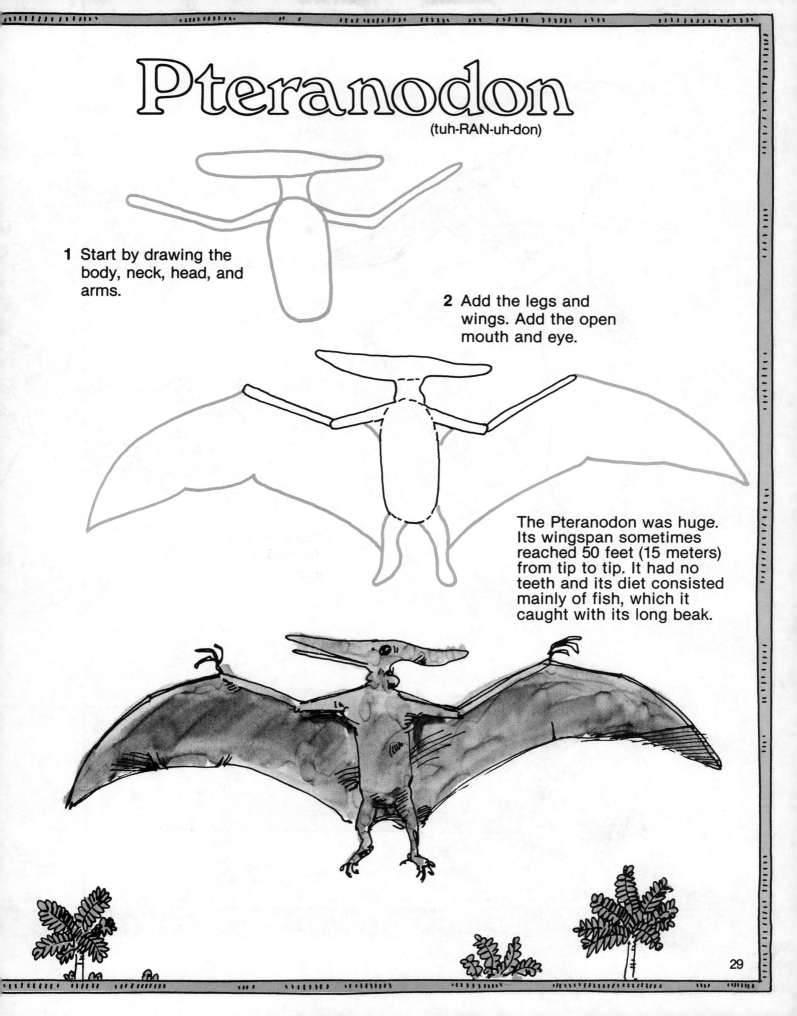

The bones of some
dinosaurs were
hollow and light.

The bones of other
dinosaurs were very big
and heavy.

The only dinosaurs we can see today look like this. But we can learn a lot from studying their skeletons. When you go to a museum, you can see how very big the dinosaurs were. Try to imagine what they looked like.

It's been a lot of fun learning to draw dinosaurs. I hope you enjoyed it as much as I did. Let's do it again soon!